Legal Notice:

Disclaimer Notice:

Table of Contents

<u>DAY 1</u>

1-Lemon Almond Poppyseed Muffins
Total Time: 50 minutes

Serving Size: 12

Ingredients:

- 1 cup almond flour
- 1 tsp lemon extract
- 1/4 cup heavy whipping cream
- 4 true lemon packets
- 2 tbsp poppy seeds
- 3 eggs
- 1/4 cup coconut oil
- 1/4 cup ricotta cheese
- 1 tsp baking powder

- 1/3 cup Truvia

Directions:

Add all ingredients into the large mixing bowl and beat until fluffy.

Spray muffin tray with cooking spray.

Pour batter into the prepared muffin tray.

Bake at 350 F/ 175 C for 40 minutes.

Serve and enjoy.

Nutritional Value (Amount per Serving):

Calories 147

Fat 12.3 g

Carbohydrates 8.3 g

Sugar 0.7 g

Protein 4.3 g

Cholesterol 46 mg

2-Crustless Cheese Pie

Total Time: 40 minutes

Serving Size: 4

Ingredients:

- 8 eggs
- 1 lb cheddar cheese, grated
- 1 1/2 cups heavy whipping cream
- Pepper
- Salt

Directions:

Preheat the oven to 400 F.

In a bowl, whisk together half cheese, eggs, whipping cream, pepper, and salt.

Spray pie dish with cooking spray.

Spread remaining half cheese into the pie dish and bake in preheated oven for 5-10 minutes or until cheese is melted.

Remove dish from oven and allow to cool slightly.

Pour egg mixture into the pie dish and bake at 350 F for 15-20 minutes or until egg is set.

Serve and enjoy.

Nutritional Value (Amount per Serving):

Calories 738

Fat 63 g

Carbohydrates 3.4 g

Sugar 1.3 g

Protein 40.2 g

Cholesterol 508 mg

3-Creamy Red Pepper Soup

Total Time: 30 minutes

Serving Size: 4

Ingredients:

- 1 cup coconut milk
- 1/8 tsp fresh thyme
- 4 cups vegetable broth
- 4 cups cauliflower florets
- 1/4 tsp red pepper flakes
- 1 tsp paprika
- 1 tbsp seasoned salt
- 1 large shallot, chopped
- 1/2 cup roasted red pepper, chopped
- 2 tbsp coconut oil

Directions:

Heat coconut oil in a pot over medium heat.

Add shallots and sauté for 3 minutes.

Add red peppers and seasoning. Stir well and cook for 2-3 minutes.

Add cauliflower, thyme, and broth. Bring to simmer.

Cover and cook for 10-15 minutes.

Using bender puree the soup until smooth.

Return soup to the stove and slowly mix in coconut milk.

Stir well and serve.

Nutritional Value (Amount per Serving):

Calories 245

Fat 20.5 g

Carbohydrates 10.4 g

Sugar 4.2 g

Protein 8.4 g

Cholesterol 0 mg

DAY 2

4-Delicious Cauliflower Hash Browns

Total Time: 25 minutes

Serving Size: 6

Ingredients:

- 1 egg
- 1/4 tsp garlic powder
- 3 cups cauliflower, grated
- 1/4 tsp cayenne pepper
- 3/4 cup cheddar cheese, shredded
- 1/8 tsp ground black pepper
- 1/2 tsp salt

Directions:

Add grated cauliflower in microwave safe bowl and microwave for 3 minutes.

Transfer cauliflower to the paper towel to soak excess liquid.

Transfer cauliflower in mixing bowl.

Add remaining ingredients into the bowl and mix well.

Make 6 equal shape hash browns from cauliflower mixture and place onto the baking tray.

Bake at 400 F for 15 minutes.

Serve and enjoy.

Nutritional Value (Amount per Serving):

Calories 81

Fat 5.5 g

Carbohydrates 3.1 g

Sugar 1.4 g

Protein 5.5 g

Cholesterol 42 mg

5-Delicious Cheddar Cheese Omelet

Total Time: 15 minutes

Serving Size: 2

Ingredients:

- 6 eggs
- 7 oz cheddar cheese, shredded
- 3 oz butter
- Pepper
- Salt

Directions:

In a bowl, whisk together eggs, half cheese, pepper, and salt.

Melt butter in a pan over medium heat.

Pour egg mixture into the pan and cook until set.

Add remaining cheese fold and serve.

Nutritional Value (Amount per Serving):

Calories 894

Fat 80.5 g

Carbohydrates 2.4 g

Sugar 1.6 g

Protein 41.7 g

Cholesterol 687 mg

6-Creamy Mushroom Soup

Total Time: 30 minutes

Serving Size: 4

Ingredients:

- 1/2 onion, diced
- 1 1/2 cup mushrooms, diced
- 1/2 tsp olive oil
- 1/4 tsp salt
- 1 tsp onion powder
- 1 2/3 cup coconut milk
- 2 cups cauliflower florets
- 1/4 tsp black pepper

Directions:

Add cauliflower, coconut milk, onion powder, pepper, and salt in a saucepan.

Cover and bring to boil over medium heat.

Reduce heat to low and simmer for 8 minutes.

Using blender puree the soup until smooth.

Heat oil in a saucepan over high heat.

Add onion and mushrooms and sauté for 8 minutes.

Add cauliflower mixture to sautéed mushrooms. Bring to boil.

Cover and simmer for 10 minutes.

Serve and enjoy.

Nutritional Value (Amount per Serving):

Calories 261

Fat 24.6 g

Carbohydrates 10.8 g

Sugar 5.8 g

Protein 4.3 g

Cholesterol 0 mg

DAY 3

7-Healthy Broccoli Cheese Nuggets

Total Time: 25 minutes

Serving Size: 4

Ingredients:

- 2 egg whites
- 1 cup cheddar cheese, shredded
- 2 cups broccoli florets
- 1/4 cup almond flour
- 1/8 tsp salt

Directions:

Preheat the oven to 350 F.

Spray a baking tray with cooking spray and set aside.

Using masher break the broccoli florets into small pieces.

Add remaining ingredients to the broccoli and mix well.

Drop 20 scoops onto baking tray and press lightly into a nugget shape.

Bake in preheated oven for 20 minutes.

Serve and enjoy.

Nutritional Value (Amount per Serving):

Calories 148

Fat 10.4 g

Carbohydrates 3.9 g

Sugar 1.1 g

Protein 10.5 g

Cholesterol 30 mg

8-Creamy Cauliflower Mash

Total Time: 15 minutes

Serving Size: 4

Ingredients:

- 1 lb cauliflower, cut into florets
- 1/2 lemon juice
- 4 oz butter
- 3 oz parmesan cheese, grated
- Pepper
- Salt

Directions:

Boil cauliflower florets in the salted water until tender.
Drain well.
Add cooked cauliflower into the blender with remaining ingredients and blend until smooth.
Serve and enjoy.

Nutritional Value (Amount per Serving):

Calories 301
Fat 27.7 g
Carbohydrates 6.9 g
Sugar 2.9 g
Protein 9.4 g
Cholesterol 76 mg

9-Cabbage Zucchini Salad

Total Time: 15 minutes

Serving Size: 10

Ingredients:

- 1 medium zucchini, spiralized
- 1 tsp stevia
- 1/3 cup rice vinegar
- 3/4 cup olive oil
- 1 cup almonds, sliced
- 1 cup sunflower seeds shelled
- 1 lb cabbage, shredded

Directions:

Chop spiralized zucchini into small pieces and set aside.

In large mixing bowl, combine together cabbage, almonds, and sunflower seeds. Stir in zucchini.

In a small bowl, mix together oil, stevia, and vinegar. Whisk well and pour over vegetables.

Toss salad well and place in refrigerator for 2 hours. Serve and enjoy.

Nutritional Value (Amount per Serving):

Calories 225

Fat 21.1 g

Carbohydrates 6.8 g

Sugar 2.3 g

Protein 3.8 g

Cholesterol 0 mg

DAY 4

10-Green Chile Cheese Breakfast Casserole

Total Time: 45 minutes

Serving Size: 8

Ingredients:

- 12 eggs, beaten
- 6 oz black olives, pitted and sliced
- 1/4 cup green onions, sliced
- 4 oz green chilies, diced
- 2 cups cheddar cheese, grated
- 2 cups cottage cheese, rinsed and drained
- Pepper
- Salt

Directions:

Preheat the oven to 375 F.

Spray casserole dish with cooking spray.

Layer cottage cheese, cheddar cheese, green chilies, green onion, and olives in the prepared casserole dish.

Whisk beaten eggs and pour over cheese mixture. Stir gently.

Season with pepper and salt.

Bake in preheated oven for 35 minutes.

Serve and enjoy.

Nutritional Value (Amount per Serving):

Calories 289

Fat 19.3 g

Carbohydrates 5.4 g

Sugar 1.4 g

Protein 23.3 g

Cholesterol 280 mg

11-Classic Zucchini Salad

Total Time: 20 minutes

Serving Size: 6

Ingredients:

- 2 lbs zucchini, peel and cut into half-inch pieces
- 1/2 tbsp Dijon mustard
- 2 tbsp fresh chives, chopped
- 1 cup mayonnaise
- 2 oz scallions, chopped
- 2 oz celery stalks, sliced
- 2 tbsp olive oil
- Pepper
- Salt

Directions:

Add zucchini pieces into the salted water and leave for 5 minutes then drain out the water well.

Fry zucchini pieces in olive oil over medium heat.

Remove pan from heat and set aside to cool.

Add remaining ingredients into the mixing bowl and mix well.

Add zucchini and mix well.

Serve and enjoy.

Nutritional Value (Amount per Serving):

Calories 310

Fat 31.7 g

Carbohydrates 6.2 g

Sugar 3 g

Protein 2.2 g

Cholesterol 13 mg

12-Delicious Keto Slaw

Total Time: 25 minutes

Serving Size: 3

Ingredients:

- 2 garlic cloves, minced
- 1 tbsp olive oil
- 2 tbsp tamari
- 1 tsp vinegar
- 1 tsp chili paste
- 1/2 cup macadamia nuts, chopped
- 4 cups green cabbage, shredded

Directions:

Toss shredded cabbage in a pan with tamari, chili paste, olive oil, and vinegar on medium-low heat.

Add garlic and stir for 1 minute.

Cover and let sit for 5 minutes.

Add chopped nuts and stir everything well to combine.

Cook for another 5 minutes.

Serve and enjoy.

Nutritional Value (Amount per Serving):

Calories 240

Fat 22 g

Carbohydrates 10.5 g

Sugar 4.7 g

Protein 4.5 g

Cholesterol 1 mg

DAY 5

13-Omelet Egg Muffins

Total Time: 35 minutes

Serving Size: 18

Ingredients:

- 12 large eggs
- 1/2 cup red bell pepper, chopped
- 1/2 cup green bell pepper, chopped
- 1/2 cup onion, chopped
- 1 1/2 cups cheddar cheese, shredded
- 3/4 cup almond milk
- 1/4 tsp ground black pepper
- 1/2 tsp salt

Directions:

Preheat the oven to 375 F.

Spray muffin tray with cooking spray and set aside.

In a large mixing bowl, whisk together eggs, almond milk, black pepper, and salt.

Stir in onion, bell peppers, and 1 cup cheese.

Pour batter into the prepared muffin tray then sprinkle remaining cheese on top.

Bake in preheated oven for 25 minutes.

Serve and enjoy.

Nutritional Value (Amount per Serving):

Calories 113

Fat 8.8 g

Carbohydrates 1.9 g

Sugar 1.1 g

Protein 6.9 g

Cholesterol 134 mg

14-Green Green Beans

Total Time: 25 minutes

Serving Size: 4

Ingredients:

- 2/3 lb fresh green beans, trim and rinse
- 1 cup heavy whipping cream
- 3 oz butter
- 1/4 tsp black pepper
- 1/2 tsp sea salt
- 1/2 lemon zest

Directions:

Heat butter in the pan over medium heat.

Add green beans to the pan and sauté for 4 minutes or until beginning to brown.

Season green beans with pepper and salt.

Add heavy cream and let simmer for 2 minutes.

Sprinkle lemon zest over the green beans.

Serve and enjoy.

Nutritional Value (Amount per Serving):

Calories 280

Fat 28.4 g

Carbohydrates 6.3 g

Sugar 1.1 g

Protein 2.2 g

Cholesterol 87 mg

15-Easy Egg Salad

Total Time: 20 minutes

Serving Size: 4

Ingredients:

- 6 hard-boiled eggs, peel and chop
- 1 tsp curry powder
- 1/2 cup mayonnaise

Directions:

Add all ingredients into the mixing bowl and toss well.
Serve and enjoy.

Nutritional Value (Amount per Serving):

Calories 211

Fat 16.4 g

Carbohydrates 7.8 g

Sugar 2.4 g

Protein 8.6 g

Cholesterol 253 mg

DAY 6

16-Spinach Mushroom Casserole

Total Time: 55 minutes

Serving Size: 8

Ingredients:

- 6 eggs, beaten
- 12 oz cheddar cheese, grated
- 16 oz cottage cheese
- 4 tbsp butter
- 2 garlic cloves, minced
- 1 onion, chopped
- 3 green onion, sliced
- 1/2 lb mushrooms, sliced
- 12 oz fresh baby spinach
- 1/2 tsp black pepper

- 1 tsp kosher salt

Directions:

Preheat the oven to 350 F.

Spray baking dish with cooking spray and set aside.

Melt butter in a pan over medium heat.

Add onion, garlic, and mushrooms and sauté for 4 minutes or until onion is softened.

Add spinach and cook until wilted, about 5 minutes.

In a separate bowl, whisk eggs, cheddar cheese, cottage cheese, pepper, and salt.

Add cooked mushroom and spinach and stir well to combine.

Pour egg mixture into the prepared baking dish.

Bake in preheated oven for 45 minutes.

Serve and enjoy.

Nutritional Value (Amount per Serving):

Calories 345

Fat 24.5 g

Carbohydrates 7.3 g

Sugar 2.1 g

Protein 25 g

Cholesterol 187 mg

17-Cabbage Dill Salad

Total Time: 25 minutes

Serving Size: 6

Ingredients:

- 2 lbs red cabbage, shred
- 2 tbsp fresh dill, chopped
- 1 orange juice
- 1 tbsp red wine vinegar
- 1 cinnamon stick
- 4 1/4 oz butter
- 1/4 tsp black pepper
- 1 tsp salt

Directions:

Heat butter in the pan over medium heat.

Add shredded cabbage to the pan and cook for 10-15 minutes.

Season with pepper and salt.

Add orange juice, vinegar, and cinnamon. Stir well and simmer for 5 minutes.

Remove pan from heat.

Add dill and lemon zest.

Serve and enjoy.

Nutritional Value (Amount per Serving):

Calories 403

Fat 39.5 g

Carbohydrates 13.1 g

Sugar 7.8 g

Protein 2.9 g

Cholesterol 104 mg

18-Mushroom Spinach Quiche

Total Time: 45 minutes

Serving Size: 6

Ingredients:

- 1 cup mozzarella cheese, shredded
- 1/2 tsp garlic powder
- 1/3 cup parmesan cheese, shredded
- 1/2 cup water
- 1/2 cup heavy cream
- 6 large eggs
- 2 provolone cheese slices
- 8 oz can mushroom, sliced
- 10 oz frozen spinach, thawed and drained
- Pepper
- Salt

Directions:

Spray pie dish with cooking spray.

Spread spinach into the prepared pie dish.

Spread sliced mushrooms over the spinach.

Arrange cheese slices over the mushrooms.

Whisk together eggs, water, and heavy cream. Mix in parmesan, pepper, garlic powder, and salt.

Pour egg mixture over spinach and mushrooms mixture.

Top with mozzarella cheese and bake at 350 F for 40 minutes.

Cut into pieces and serve.

Nutritional Value (Amount per Serving):

Calories 227

Fat 15.8 g

Carbohydrates 4.6 g

Sugar 0.7 g

Protein 17.3 g

Cholesterol 218 mg

DAY 7

19-Healthy Overnight Oats

Total Time: 10 minutes

Serving Size: 2

Ingredients:

- 1/2 cup harvest hemp hearts
- 1 tbsp chia seed
- 2/3 cup coconut milk
- 4 drops liquid stevia
- 1/2 tsp vanilla extract
- Pinch of salt

Directions:

Add all ingredients into the large container and stir well.

Fat 98 g
Carbohydrates 12.1 g
Sugar 5.5 g
Protein 5.5 g
Cholesterol 259 mg

21-Baked Egg Skillet

Total Time: 30 minutes

Serving Size: 3

Ingredients:

- 4 eggs
- 1 ripe avocado, sliced
- 10 oz Rotel tomatoes
- Pepper
- Salt

Directions:

Preheat the oven to 400 F.

Spray medium pan with cooking spray.

Add tomatoes to the pan and simmer over medium heat.

Arrange sliced avocado over the tomatoes in a circle.

Slowly put each egg between the avocado slices.

Season with black pepper and salt.

Place pan in preheated oven and bake for 10 minutes.

Serve and enjoy.

Nutritional Value (Amount per Serving):

Calories 235

Fat 19 g

Carbohydrates 9.7 g

Sugar 0.8 g

Protein 9.3 g

Cholesterol 218 mg

DAY 8

22-Asparagus Cheese Quiche

Total Time: 45 minutes

Serving Size: 6

Ingredients:

- 4 eggs
- 4 egg whites
- 2 tbsp feta cheese, crumbled
- 1 cup cottage cheese
- 1/2 tsp dried thyme
- 1/4 cup water
- 8 oz asparagus, cut into 1-inch pieces
- 1/4 tsp ground black pepper
- 1/4 tsp salt

Directions:

Preheat the oven to 375 F.

Spray baking dish with cooking spray and set aside.

Add water into the large pot and bring to boil over high heat.

Add asparagus into the pot and cook for 2 minutes.

Drain and rinse with cold water.

In a large bowl, whisk together egg whites, eggs, cottage cheese, thyme, water, pepper, and salt.

Pour egg mixture into the prepared dish.

Sprinkle asparagus pieces into the egg mixture then top with feta cheese.

Bake in preheated oven for 30 minutes.

Cut into pieces and serve.

Nutritional Value (Amount per Serving):

Calories 102

Fat 5 g

Carbohydrates 4 g

Sugar 3 g

Protein 11 g

Cholesterol 116 mg

23-Tomato Cheese Salad

Total Time: 10 minutes

Serving Size: 4

Ingredients:

- 2 tbsp green pesto
- 8 oz mozzarella, mini cheese balls, cut in half
- 8 oz cherry tomatoes. cut in half
- Pepper
- Salt

Directions:

Add tomato, cheese, and pesto into the bowl and mix well.

Season with pepper and salt.

Serve and enjoy.

Nutritional Value (Amount per Serving):

Calories 182

Fat 11.2 g

Carbohydrates 4.4 g

Sugar 1.5 g

Protein 16.8 g

Cholesterol 31 mg

24-Artichoke Spinach Casserole

Total Time: 40 minutes

Serving Size: 12

Ingredients:

- 16 large eggs
- 1/2 tsp red pepper, crushed
- 1/2 tsp thyme, diced
- 1 garlic cloves, minced
- 1/4 cup onion, shaved
- 1/2 cup ricotta cheese
- 1/2 cup parmesan cheese
- 1 cup cheddar cheese, shredded
- 10 oz frozen spinach, thawed and drain well
- 14 oz can artichoke hearts, drained and cut into pieces

- 1/4 cup coconut milk
- 1 tsp salt

Directions:

Preheat the oven to 350 F.

Spray baking dish with cooking spray.

In a large bowl, whisk together eggs and coconut milk.

Add spinach and artichoke into the egg mixture.

Add all remaining ingredients except ricotta cheese and stir well to combine.

Pour egg mixture into the prepared baking dish.

Spread ricotta cheese evenly over the egg mixture.

Bake in preheated oven for 30 minutes.

Serve warm and enjoy.

Nutritional Value (Amount per Serving):

Calories 205

Fat 13.7 g

Carbohydrates 4.9 g

Sugar 1.5 g

Protein 15.9 g

Cholesterol 266 mg

DAY 9

25-Spinach Avocado Cheese Omelet

Total Time: 25 minutes

Serving Size: 2

Ingredients:

- 3 eggs
- 1/2 avocado, diced
- 2 tbsp goat cheese, crumble
- 1 cup baby spinach
- 3 oz mushrooms, sliced
- 1 tbsp olive oil
- Pepper
- Salt

Directions:

Heat olive oil in a pan over medium heat.

Add sliced mushrooms and cook about 5 minutes or until tender.

Transfer mushrooms in a bowl.

Clean pan with a paper towel then sprays with cooking spray and heat over medium heat.

In a small bowl, whisk together eggs, pepper, and salt.

Pour egg mixture into the hot pan and cook until edges are set and lightly brown, about 6 minutes.

Arrange sautéed mushrooms, avocado, goat cheese, and spinach on half omelet then fold another half over the veggies.

Serve and enjoy.

Nutritional Value (Amount per Serving):

Calories 325

Fat 28 g

Carbohydrates 7.3 g

Sugar 2.1 g

Protein 14 g

Cholesterol 258 mg

26-Mix Vegetable Salad

Total Time: 15 minutes

Serving Size: 10

Ingredients:

- 2 cups carrots, chopped
- 2 cups cherry tomatoes, halved
- 2 cups cauliflower florets
- 1 bell pepper, seeded and chopped
- 1 cucumber, seeded and chopped
- For dressing:
- 4 tsp Dijon mustard
- 2 tbsp shallots, minced
- 1/2 cup red wine vinegar
- 2 garlic cloves, minced
- 2 tsp Italian seasoning

Directions:

Heat butter and olive oil into the pan over medium heat.

Add garlic and mushrooms and sauté until tender.

Add heavy cream, Italian seasoning, cream cheese, parmesan cheese, pepper, and salt. Stir until sauce smooth.

Serve and enjoy.

Nutritional Value (Amount per Serving):

Calories 272

Fat 25.1 g

Carbohydrates 3.4 g

Sugar 1.1 g

Protein 11.3 g

Cholesterol 68 mg

DAY 10

28-Cheese Spinach Egg Bake

Total Time: 45 minutes

Serving Size: 6

Ingredients:

- 8 eggs, beaten
- 1 tsp spike seasoning
- 1/3 cup green onion, sliced
- 1 1/2 cups mozzarella
- 1 tsp olive oil
- 5 oz fresh spinach
- Pepper
- Salt

Directions:

Preheat the oven to 375 F.

Spray casserole dish with cooking spray and set aside.

Heat oil in a large pan over medium heat.

Add spinach and cook until wilted, about 2 minutes.

Transfer cooked spinach into the casserole dish and spread well.

Spread onion and cheese onto the spinach layer.

In a small bowl, whisk together eggs, pepper, spike seasoning, and salt.

Pour egg mixture over spinach mixture and stir gently.

Bake in preheated oven for 35 minutes.

Cut into pieces and serve.

Nutritional Value (Amount per Serving):

Calories 118

Fat 8 g

Carbohydrates 2 g

Sugar 0.7 g

Protein 10.2 g

Cholesterol 222 mg

29-Cucumber Onion Salad

Total Time: 10 minutes

Serving Size: 4

Ingredients:

- 2 large cucumbers, sliced
- 4 tbsp white vinegar
- 1/4 cup sour cream
- 1 garlic clove, grated
- 1 tbsp dill, chopped
- 1/4 cup red onion, sliced
- Pepper
- Salt

Directions:

Add all ingredients into the large bowl and mix until well combined.

Place salad bowl in refrigerator for 30 minutes.

Serve chilled and enjoy.

Nutritional Value (Amount per Serving):

Calories 63

Fat 3.2 g

Carbohydrates 7.6 g

Sugar 2.9 g

Protein 1.7 g

Cholesterol 6 mg

30-Basil Cheese Green Beans

Total Time: 20 minutes
Serving Size: 3

Ingredients:

- 1 lb fresh green beans, trimmed
- 2 tbsp parmesan cheese, grated
- 3/4 tsp dried basil
- 1 tbsp olive oil
- 1/4 tsp black pepper
- 1/4 tsp salt

Directions:

Preheat the oven to 425 F.

Spread green beans onto the baking tray. Toss with olive oil.

Season with basil, pepper, and salt.

Roast in preheated oven for 10 minutes.

Sprinkle with parmesan cheese and serve.

Nutritional Value (Amount per Serving):

Calories 112
Fat 6.4 g
Carbohydrates 10.9 g
Sugar 2.1 g
Protein 4.8 g
Cholesterol 5 mg

DAY 11

31-Delicious Cheese Fritters

Total Time: 15 minutes

Serving Size: 6

Ingredients:

- 3 tbsp olive oil

- 2 eggs

- 1 lemon zest

- 2 tbsp fresh oregano, chopped

- 1 1/2 tbsp coconut flour

- 1/2 cup parmesan cheese, grated

- 1 lb fresh ricotta cheese

- 12 tsp black pepper

- Pinch of salt

Directions:

Add all ingredients except olive oil into the bowl and mix well until combined.

Make 12 small patties from mixture.

Heat olive oil in a large pan over medium heat.

Place fritters onto the hot pan and cook for 2-3 minutes on each side or until lightly golden brown.

Serve and enjoy.

Nutritional Value (Amount per Serving):

Calories 229

Fat 16.7 g

Carbohydrates 7.1 g

Sugar 0.7 g

Protein 13.8 g

Cholesterol 83 mg

32-Zucchini Pasta Salad

Total Time: 25 minutes

Serving Size: 2

Ingredients:

- 1 yellow zucchini, cut into julienned
- 1 green zucchini, cut into julienned
- 3 tbsp parmesan cheese, grated
- 1 fresh lemon zest, grated
- 1 tbsp fresh lemon juice
- 1 1/2 tbsp olive oil
- Pepper
- Salt

Directions:

In a bowl, whisk together olive oil, lemon zest, pepper, salt, and lemon juice.

Add zucchini in a bowl and toss until well coated.

Add parmesan cheese and toss to combine.

Serve and enjoy.

Nutritional Value (Amount per Serving):

Calories 123

Fat 10.9 g

Carbohydrates 6.8 g

Sugar 3.6 g

Protein 2.4 g

Cholesterol 0 mg

33-Healthy Brussels sprouts

Total Time: 10 minutes

Serving Size: 1

Ingredients:

- 6 Brussels sprouts, trimmed and cut in half
- 1 tbsp parmesan cheese, grated
- 1 tsp olive oil
- 1/2 tsp apple cider vinegar
- 1/8 tsp black pepper
- Pinch of salt

Directions:

Add Brussels sprouts, olive oil, apple cider vinegar, black pepper, and salt into the mixing bowl and toss well.

Sprinkle parmesan cheese and combine well.

Serve and enjoy.

Nutritional Value (Amount per Serving):

Calories 112

Fat 6.5 g

Carbohydrates 10.9 g

Sugar 2.5 g

Protein 5.8 g

Cholesterol 4 mg

DAY 12

34-Almond Coconut Pancake

Total Time: 25 minutes

Serving Size: 11

Ingredients:

- 6 large eggs
- 1 tsp vanilla extract
- 6 tbsp almond milk, unsweetened
- 1 tsp baking powder
- 2 tbsp erythritol
- 1/4 cup coconut flour
- 1 cup almond flour
- Pinch of salt

Directions:

Whisk all ingredients in the mixing bowl until smooth.

Heat pan over medium-low heat.

Pour batter into hot pan and make small pancakes.

Cover and cook about 2-3 minutes then flip to another side and cook for 1-2 minutes or until golden brown.

Repeat with remaining batter.

Serve and enjoy.

Nutritional Value (Amount per Serving):

Calories 101

Fat 8 g

Carbohydrates 5.5 g

Sugar 3.4 g

Protein 5.7 g

Cholesterol 101 mg

35-Creamy Garlic Cauliflower Mashed

Total Time: 30 minutes

Serving Size: 4

Ingredients:

- 1 large cauliflower head, cut into florets
- 2 tbsp parmesan cheese, grated
- 3 garlic cloves
- 2 tbsp goat cheese
- Pepper
- Salt

Directions:

Add cauliflower, garlic, and salt in a saucepan and pour enough water in saucepan to cover the cauliflower.

Boil cauliflower over low heat for 20 minutes or until soft.

Remove cauliflower from heat and drain.

Add drained cauliflower in food processor and process until pureed.

Add cauliflower puree in a pan and cook over low heat.

Add goat cheese, parmesan cheese, pepper, and salt.

Stir well.

Cook for 3 minutes.

Serve and enjoy.

Nutritional Value (Amount per Serving):

Calories 32

Fat 0.1 g

Carbohydrates 6.8 g

Sugar 2.7 g

Protein 2.4 g

Cholesterol 0 mg

36-Delicious Taco Salad

Total Time: 15 minutes

Serving Size: 4

Ingredients:

- 4 cups iceberg lettuce, chopped
- 1/2 avocado, sliced
- 1/2 cup hemp seeds
- 1/2 tbsp chili powder
- 1/2 cup macadamia nuts
- 1/2 cup almonds
- 1 cup salsa
- Pepper
- Salt

Directions:

In a large bowl, add macadamia nuts and almonds.

Cover nuts with water and soak for 2 hours. Drain well.

Add soaked nuts and chili powder into the food processor and grind them into a coarse.

Add hemp seed into the nut mixture and stir well.

Add nut mixture into the mixing bowl with remaining ingredients and toss well.

Serve and enjoy.

Nutritional Value (Amount per Serving):

Calories 334

Fat 30.10 g

Carbohydrates 3.95 g

Sugar 4 g

Protein 11.6 g

Cholesterol 0 mg

DAY 13

37-Roasted Vegetable Frittata

Total Time: 40 minutes

Serving Size: 2

Ingredients:

- 1/2 beet, peel and sliced
- 2 tsp olive oil
- 1/3 cup broccoli florets
- 1/2 yellow bell pepper, sliced
- 4 egg whites
- 1/2 tsp oregano
- 2 tbsp cheese, grated
- 1/2 tsp sea salt

Directions:

Coat vegetables with 1 tsp olive oil and salt.

Arrange vegetables onto the baking tray and grill at 180 C for 15 minutes.

In another bowl, whisk together egg whites, oregano and salt.

Heat remaining olive oil in a pan over medium heat.

Spread roasted vegetables onto the pan then pour egg mixture over the vegetables.

Spread cheese on top of egg and vegetable mixture.

Cover and cook on low heat for 10 minutes or until set.

Serve and enjoy.

Nutritional Value (Amount per Serving):

Calories 273

Fat 19.1 g

Carbohydrates 6.1 g

Sugar 3.8 g

Protein 20.8 g

Cholesterol 47 mg

38-Yummy Cauliflower Soup

Total Time: 35 minutes

Serving Size: 4

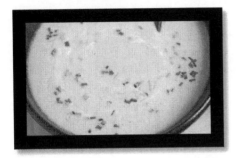

Ingredients:

- 1/2 head cauliflower, diced
- 1 garlic clove, minced
- 16 oz vegetable broth
- 1 small onion, diced
- 1/4 tbsp olive oil
- 1/2 tsp salt

Directions:

Heat olive oil in a saucepan over medium heat.

Add onion and garlic in a saucepan and cook for 4 minutes.

Add cauliflower and broth. Stir well and bring to boil.

Cover pan with lid and simmer for 15 minutes.

Season with salt.

Using blender puree the soup until smooth and creamy.

Serve and enjoy.

Nutritional Value (Amount per Serving):

Calories 42

Fat 1.6 g

Carbohydrates 4.1 g

Sugar 1.9 g

Protein 3.2 g

Cholesterol 0 mg

39-Creamy Celery Soup

Total Time: 40 minutes

Serving Size: 4

Ingredients:

- 6 large celery stalks, chopped
- 1 tbsp lime juice
- 1 tsp dried dill
- 2 cups water
- 1 tsp olive oil
- 1 cup coconut milk
- 1 onion, sliced
- 1/2 tsp black pepper
- 1 tsp salt

Directions:

Heat olive oil in a saucepan over medium heat.

Add onion and sauté for 3-4 minutes.

Add celery and cook for 3 minutes.

Add water and salt and simmer for 30 minutes over medium heat.

Using blender puree the soup until smooth.

Again simmer for 5 minutes.

Season with lemon juice, pepper, and dill.

Serve hot and enjoy.

Nutritional Value (Amount per Serving):

Calories 178

Fat 15.7 g

Carbohydrates 10 g

Sugar 4.7 g

Protein 2.5 g

Cholesterol 0 mg

DAY 14

40-Avocado Egg Baked

Total Time: 25 minutes

Serving Size: 6

Ingredients:

- 3 avocados, halved and seeded
- 2 tbsp fresh chives, chopped
- 6 large eggs
- 1/4 tsp red pepper flakes
- 1/4 tsp ground black pepper
- 1/4 tsp salt

Directions:

Preheat the oven to 425 F.

Spray a baking tray with cooking spray and set aside.

Scoop out about 2 tbsp flesh of avocado to creating a small hole in the center of each avocado.

Gently break 1 egg into the hole of avocado.

Season with red pepper flakes, pepper, and salt.

Repeat same with remaining avocado and egg.

Place prepared avocado egg onto the baking tray and bake in preheated oven for 15-20 minutes or until egg white set.

Garnish with chopped chives and serve.

Nutritional Value (Amount per Serving):

Calories 277

Fat 24.6 g

Carbohydrates 9.2 g

Sugar 0.9 g

Protein 8.3 g

Cholesterol 186 mg

41-Cheese Egg Dill Salad

Total Time: 15 minutes

Serving Size: 2

Ingredients:

- 3 eggs, hard-boiled
- 1 tsp mustard
- 3 oz cottage cheese
- 1 tbsp dill cubes
- 1 tbsp onion, chopped
- Pepper
- Salt

Directions:

Chop boiled eggs.

Add all ingredients into the bowl and mix well.

Serve and enjoy.

Nutritional Value (Amount per Serving):

Calories 143

Fat 7.9 g

Carbohydrates 3.1 g

Sugar 1 g

Protein 14.6 g

Cholesterol 249 mg

42-Kale Avocado Salad

Total Time: 30 minutes

Serving Size: 2

Ingredients:

- 1 medium avocado, peel and cut into cubes
- 2 tbsp pine nuts
- 2 tbsp olive oil
- 1/2 small orange juice
- 1/2 lime juice
- 2 cups kale, chopped
- 1/4 tsp black pepper
- 1/2 tsp sea salt

Directions:

Heat 2-liter water into the pot.

Add salt and kale into the pot and cook for 10-20 minutes.

Drain kale well and set aside to cool.

Add kale, avocado, and pine nuts into the mixing bowl and toss well.

Season salad with pepper and salt.

In a small bowl, mix together oil, orange juice, and lime juice and pour over salad.

Serve and enjoy.

Nutritional Value (Amount per Serving):

Calories 379

Fat 34 g

Carbohydrates 9.8 g

Sugar 3 g

Protein 5.3 g

Cholesterol 0 mg

DAY 15

43-Breakfast English Muffins

Total Time: 10 minutes

Serving Size: 2

Ingredients:

- 1 egg, beaten
- 1 tbsp almond milk, unsweetened
- 1/2 tsp baking powder
- 2 tbsp almond flour
- 1 tbsp butter
- 2 tbsp almond butter
- 1/8 tsp salt

Directions:

Spray ramekin with cooking spray and set aside.

Melt butter and almond butter in microwave safe dish and set aside to cool.

In a small bowl, whisk together almond flour, baking powder, and salt.

Pour egg and milk into the dry ingredients and stir until well combined. Add both melted butter and mix well.

Pour mixture into the prepared ramekin and microwave for 2 minutes.

Serve and enjoy.

Nutritional Value (Amount per Serving):

Calories 223

Fat 20.6 g

Carbohydrates 5.3 g

Sugar 1.1 g

Protein 7.8 g

Cholesterol 97 mg

44-Creamy Egg Stuffed Cucumber

Total Time: 15 minutes

Serving Size: 4

Ingredients:

- 1 large cucumber, 12 inch
- 1/4 cup plain yogurt
- 1/8 tsp cayenne pepper
- 1/4 tsp ground pepper
- 2 tsp Dijon mustard
- 4 eggs, hard-boiled and peeled
- 1 celery stalk, diced
- 2 tbsp parsley, chopped
- 1/8 tsp salt

Directions:

In a mixing bowl, mash eggs with a fork.

Add parsley, celery, yogurt, mustard, pepper, and salt. Stir well.

Cut cucumber in half then cut each piece in half lengthwise.

Scoop out cucumber seeds.

Divide the eggs mixture into the 4 equal portions and stuffed in four cucumber boats.

Sprinkle cayenne pepper over the top of each stuffed cucumber.

Serve immediately and enjoy.

Nutritional Value (Amount per Serving):

Calories 89

Fat 4.8 g

Carbohydrates 4.6 g

Sugar 2.8 g

Protein 7.1 g

Cholesterol 165 mg

45-Stuff Bell Pepper

Total Time: 35 minutes

Serving Size: 4

Ingredients:

- 2 medium bell peppers, cut in half and deseeded
- 2 tbsp olive oil
- 1/4 cup baby broccoli florets
- 1/4 cup cherry tomatoes
- 1 tsp dried sage
- 2.5 oz cheddar cheese, grated
- 4 eggs
- 7 oz almond milk
- Pepper
- Salt

Directions:

Preheat the oven to 390 F.

In a bowl, whisk together eggs, milk, broccoli, cherry tomatoes, sage, pepper, and salt.

Add olive oil to the baking dish and spread well.

Place bell pepper halves in the baking dish.

Pour egg mixture into the bell pepper halves.

Sprinkle cheese on top of bell pepper.

Bake in preheated oven for 25 minutes.

Serve and enjoy.

Nutritional Value (Amount per Serving):

Calories 285

Fat 25.2 g

Carbohydrates 5.8 g

Sugar 3.3 g

Protein 11.5 g

Cholesterol 167 mg

DAY 16

46-Coconut Flatbread

Total Time: 20 minutes

Serving Size: 3

Ingredients:

- 3 egg whites
- 1/2 tsp garlic powder
- 1/2 tsp onion powder
- 1 tbsp water
- 2 tbsp coconut milk
- 1/4 tsp baking powder
- 2 tbsp coconut flour
- 1 tbsp butter

Directions:

Add all ingredients into the mixing bowl and whisk until smooth.

Heat pan over medium heat.

Add butter to the hot pan.

Once butter is melted then pour batter into the hot pan and spread with spatula.

Cook until edges are lightly brown then flip to another side and cook until lightly golden brown.

Repeat same with remaining ingredients.

Serve and enjoy.

Nutritional Value (Amount per Serving):

Calories 84

Fat 3.8 g

Carbohydrates 7 g

Sugar 1.5 g

Protein 5.3 g

Cholesterol 0 mg

47-Delicious Eggplant Zucchini with Cheese

Total Time: 50 minutes

Serving Size: 6

Ingredients:

- 1 medium eggplant, sliced
- 1 tbsp olive oil
- 1 cup cherry tomatoes, halved
- 4 garlic cloves, minced
- 4 tbsp parsley, chopped
- 4 tbsp basil, chopped
- 3 medium zucchini, sliced
- 3 oz Parmesan cheese, grated
- 1/4 tsp pepper
- 1/4 tsp salt

Directions:

Preheat the oven to 350 F.

Spray baking dish with non-stick cooking spray.

In a mixing bowl, add chopped cherry tomatoes, eggplant, zucchini, olive oil, garlic, cheese, basil, pepper and salt toss well until combined.

Transfer the eggplant mixture into the baking dish and place dish in the oven.

Bake for 35 minutes or until vegetables are tender.

Garnish with chopped parsley and serve.

Nutritional Value (Amount per Serving):

Calories 110

Fat 5.8 g

Carbohydrates 10.4 g

Sugar 4.8 g

Protein 7.0 g

Cholesterol 10 mg

48-Healthy Garlic Spinach

Total Time: 15 minutes

Serving Size: 2

Ingredients:

- 1 bunch fresh spinach, wash and dry
- 4 garlic cloves, sliced
- 1 tbsp olive oil
- Pepper
- Salt

Directions:

Heat oil in the pan over medium heat.

Add garlic and cook for 5 minutes.

Add spinach and cook until wilted, about 2 minutes.

Season with pepper and salt.

Serve and enjoy.

Nutritional Value (Amount per Serving):

Calories 108

Fat 7.7 g

Carbohydrates 8.2 g
Sugar 0.8 g
Protein 5.3 g
Cholesterol 0 mg

DAY 17

49-Spinach Cauliflower Bread

Total Time: 25 minutes

Serving Size: 7

Ingredients:

- 1 cauliflower head, cut into florets
- 2 garlic cloves, crushed
- 2 eggs
- 1 cup spinach
- 1/2 onion, diced
- 1 tbsp coconut oil
- Pepper
- Salt

Directions:

Add cauliflower into the food processor and process until it resembles breadcrumbs.

Add oil to the pan and heat over medium heat.

Add cauliflower, onion, and garlic to the pan and sauté for 10 minutes.

Beat eggs in a bowl and add cauliflower and remaining ingredients. Stir well.

Spray a baking tray with cooking spray.

Spoon cauliflower mixture into rounds onto the prepared tray and bake at 350 F for 15 minutes.

Serve and enjoy.

Nutritional Value (Amount per Serving):

Calories 50

Fat 3.3 g

Carbohydrates 3.3 g

Sugar 1.4 g

Protein 2.6 g

Cholesterol 47 mg

50-Tasty Egg Veggie Scramble

Total Time: 20 minutes

Serving Size: 1

Ingredients:

- 3 eggs, beaten
- 1/2 cup spinach, chopped
- 1/4 cup bell peppers, chopped
- 4 Bella mushrooms, sliced
- 1 tbsp coconut oil
- Pepper
- Salt

Directions:

Melt half tbsp of coconut oil in a pan over medium heat.

Add vegetables and sauté for 5 minutes.

Heat remaining oil in another pan and add beaten eggs into the pan and cook over medium heat, stirring constantly to prevent overcooking.

Season cooked eggs with pepper and salt.

Add sautéed vegetables to egg mixture and mix well.

Serve and enjoy.

Nutritional Value (Amount per Serving):

Calories 323

Fat 26.9 g

Carbohydrates 4.5 g

Sugar 2.9 g

Protein 17.9 g

Cholesterol 491 mg

51-Creamy Broccoli Soup

Total Time: 25 minutes

Serving Size: 3

Ingredients:

- 4 cup broccoli florets
- 1/2 tsp ground nutmeg
- 1 small avocado, peel and sliced
- 2 cups vegetable broth

Directions:

Add broth into the pot and bring to simmer over medium-high heat.

Add broccoli into the pot and cook for 8 minutes or until tender.

Reduce heat to low and add avocado and nutmeg. Stir well and cooks continue for 4 minutes.

Using blender puree the soup until smooth.

Serve and enjoy.

Nutritional Value (Amount per Serving):

Calories 206

Fat 14.5 g

Carbohydrates 14 g

Sugar 3 g

Protein 8 g

Cholesterol 0 mg

DAY 18

52-Cheesy Zucchini Muffins

Total Time: 28 minutes

Serving Size: 8

Ingredients:

- 4 eggs
- 1/4 cup cheddar cheese, grated
- 1 tbsp thyme
- 1 tbsp oregano
- 1/2 tsp baking powder
- 1/2 cup parmesan cheese, grated
- 1/3 cup coconut flour
- 1/4 cup water
- 1/4 cup butter, melted

- 1 1/2 cups zucchini, grated
- 1/4 tsp salt

Directions:

Preheat the oven to 400 F.

In a bowl, whisk eggs, water, and butter.

Add coconut flour, baking powder, and salt. Mix well.

Add zucchini, oregano, and thyme

Add cheese and mix well.

Pour batter into muffin cups and sprinkle with remaining cheese.

Bake in preheated oven for 15 minutes.

Serve and enjoy.

Nutritional Value (Amount per Serving):

Calories 141

Fat 10.9 g

Carbohydrates 5 g

Sugar 0.6 g

Protein 6.7 g

Cholesterol 105 mg

53-Caesar Salad

Total Time: 20 minutes

Serving Size: 4

Ingredients:

- 2 tsp Dijon mustard
- 1 tbsp capers
- 1 tbsp caper brine
- 3 garlic cloves, minced
- 12 cups romaine lettuce, chopped
- 4 tbsp hemp seeds
- 2 tbsp water
- 3 tbsp fresh lemon juice
- 1 ripe avocado
- Pepper
- Salt

Directions:

Add avocado, pepper, salt, mustard, capers, caper brine, garlic, water, and lemon juice in a blender and blend until smooth.

Pour avocado mixture and hemp seeds in large mixing bowl and mix well.

Add chopped romaine lettuce in a bowl and toss well. Serve and enjoy.

Nutritional Value (Amount per Serving):

Calories 168

Fat 12.5 g

Carbohydrates 5.2 g

Sugar 3.9 g

Protein 6.6 g

Cholesterol 0 mg

54-Garlic Zucchini Soup

Total Time: 30 minutes

Serving Size: 4

Ingredients:

- 2 lbs zucchini, chopped
- 1/4 cup fresh basil leaves
- 3 cup vegetable stock
- 1 tbsp butter
- 2 garlic cloves, minced
- 3/4 cup onion, chopped
- 1 tsp salt

Directions:

Heat butter in the pan over medium heat.

Add garlic and onion and sauté for 5 minutes.

Add zucchini and salt and cook for 5 minutes.

Add vegetable stock and simmer for 15 minutes.

Stir in basil.

Using blender puree the soup until smooth.

Serve and enjoy.

Nutritional Value (Amount per Serving):

Calories 80

Fat 4.5 g

Carbohydrates 10.7 g

Sugar 5.4 g

Protein 3.1 g

Cholesterol 0 mg

DAY 19

55-Delicious Zucchini Quiche

Total Time: 50 minutes

Serving Size: 6

Ingredients:

- 3 eggs
- 1/2 tsp dried oregano
- 1/2 tsp dried basil
- 1 tbsp olive oil
- 1 cup mozzarella, shredded
- 15 oz ricotta
- 1 onion, chopped
- 2 medium zucchini, sliced
- Black pepper

- Salt

Directions:

Preheat the oven to 350 F.

Sauté zucchini over low heat.

Add onion and cook for 10 minutes or until tender.

Add pepper and seasoning to zucchini mixture.

Beat eggs, and then add in mozzarella and ricotta. Fold in onions and zucchini.

Spray pie dish with cooking spray.

Pour egg mixture into the pie dish and bake in preheated oven for 30 minutes.

Serve and enjoy.

Nutritional Value (Amount per Serving):

Calories 181

Fat 11.1 g

Carbohydrates 8 g

Sugar 2.3 g

Protein 13.2 g

Cholesterol 106 mg

56-Delicious Broccoli Omelet

Total Time: 20 minutes

Serving Size: 2

Ingredients:

- 1 cup broccoli, chopped and cooked
- 1 tbsp olive oil
- 4 eggs
- 1/4 tsp pepper
- 1 tbsp parsley, chopped
- 1/4 tsp marjoram, dried
- 1/2 tsp salt

Directions:

In a bowl, beat eggs with pepper, marjoram, and salt.

Heat olive oil in a pan over medium heat.

Pour broccoli and eggs mixture into the hot pan and cook until set then flip the omelet and cook until lightly golden brown.

Garnish with chopped parsley.

Serve hot and enjoy.

Nutritional Value (Amount per Serving):

Calories 203

Fat 15.9 g

Carbohydrates 4 g

Sugar 1.5 g

Protein 12.4 g

Cholesterol 327 mg

57-Creamy Cauliflower Green Soup

Total Time: 45 minutes

Serving Size: 4

Ingredients:

- 4 cups cauliflower florets, chopped
- 2 tbsp butter
- 1/2 cup coconut milk
- 2 cups water
- 4 cups vegetable broth
- 1 tsp curry powder
- 4 garlic cloves, minced
- 1 small onion, chopped
- 3 cups baby spinach, chopped
- 1 bunch chard, chopped

Directions:

Melt butter in the saucepan over medium heat.

Add onion and sauté until softened.

Add garlic and sauté for a minute.

Add curry powder and sauté for a minute.

Meanwhile, heat cauliflower and vegetable broth in a pot over medium heat. Bring to simmer for 10 minutes.

Add water and chard and simmer for another 10 minutes.

Remove from heat and stir in coconut milk and add sautéed garlic, onion and spices.

Using blender puree the soup until smooth.

Season soup with pepper and salt.

Serve and enjoy.

Nutritional Value (Amount per Serving):

Calories 211

Fat 15.6 g

Carbohydrates 12 g

Sugar 5.1 g

Protein 8.8 g

Cholesterol 0 mg

DAY 20

58-Healthy Cinnamon Flax Seed Porridge

Total Time: 10 minutes
Serving Size: 1

Ingredients:

- 1 cup water
- 4 tbsp coconut milk
- 4 tbsp flaxseed
- 1/8 tsp cinnamon

Directions:

Add all ingredients into the microwave safe bowl and mix well.

Cook on high for 2 minutes.

Serve and enjoy.

Nutritional Value (Amount per Serving):

Calories 286

Fat 23.1 g

Carbohydrates 11.3 g

Sugar 2.4 g

Protein 6.6 g

Cholesterol 0 mg

59-Perfect Egg Avocado Salad

Total Time: 15 minutes

Serving Size: 2

Ingredients:

- 3 hard-boiled eggs, chopped
- 1 tbsp parsley, chopped
- 1/4 tsp dill weed
- 1/4 tsp garlic powder
- 1 tbsp apple cider vinegar
- 1 tsp Dijon mustard
- 1/2 large avocado
- 1/4 tsp salt

Directions:

Add avocado into the mixing bowl and mash well.

Add remaining ingredients and mix well.

Serve and enjoy.

Nutritional Value (Amount per Serving):

Calories 202

Fat 16.5 g

Carbohydrates 5.5 g

Sugar 0.9 g

Protein 9.5 g

Cholesterol 246 mg

60-Healthy Garlic Swiss chard

Total Time: 15 minutes

Serving Size: 4

Ingredients:

- 8 cups Swiss chard, trimmed and cut into 1/2 inch pieces
- 1/2 lemon juice
- 1/4 tsp red pepper, crushed
- 2 garlic cloves, minced
- 1 1/2 tbsp olive oil
- 1 1/2 tbsp butter
- Pepper
- Salt

Directions:

Melt butter in a pan over medium-low heat.

Add garlic and red pepper and sauté for 1 minute.

Add Swiss chard stir well.

Cover and cook for 8 minutes or until tender.

Add lemon juice and season with pepper and salt.

Serve and enjoy.

Nutritional Value (Amount per Serving):

Calories 103

Fat 9.9 g

Carbohydrates 3.9 g

Sugar 1.3 g

Protein 1.6 g

Cholesterol 11 mg

DAY 21

61-Perfect Breakfast Waffles

Total Time: 30 minutes

Serving Size: 5

Ingredients:

- 5 eggs, separated
- 1/2 cup butter, melted
- 3 tbsp almond milk
- 2 tsp vanilla extract
- 1 tsp baking powder
- 4 tbsp granulated sweetener
- 4 tbsp coconut flour

Directions:

Add egg whites into the bowl and whisk until stiff peaks form.

In another bowl, mix together egg yolks, baking powder, sweetener, and coconut flour.

Slowly add melted butter and mix until smooth.

Add vanilla and almond milk and mix well.

Gently fold egg white mixture into the egg yolk mixture.

Pour enough waffle mixture into the hot waffle maker and cook waffle until golden from both the sides.

Repeat same with remaining mixture.

Serve and enjoy.

Nutritional Value (Amount per Serving):

Calories 280

Fat 26 g

Carbohydrates 4.5 g

Sugar 1.4 g

Protein 7 g

Cholesterol 214 mg

62-Tasty Pumpkin Spiced Soup

Total Time: 55 minutes

Serving Size: 4

Ingredients:

- 1 cup pumpkin puree
- 1/2 tsp ginger, minced
- 2 garlic cloves, minced
- 1/4 onion, chopped
- 4 tbsp butter
- 1 1/2 cups vegetable broth
- 1/2 cup heavy cream
- 1 bay leaf
- 1/8 tsp nutmeg
- 1/4 tsp coriander
- 1/4 tsp cinnamon

- 1/2 tsp pepper
- 1/2 tsp salt

Directions:

Melt butter in a saucepan over medium-low heat.

Add ginger, garlic, and onion to the pan and sauté for 2-3 minutes.

Add spices and stir well and cook for 2 minutes.

Add broth and pumpkin puree and mix well. Bring to boil then reduce heat to low and simmer for 20 minutes.

Using blender puree the soup until smooth then simmer for another 20 minutes.

Remove pan from heat and add heavy cream and stir well.

Serve and enjoy.

Nutritional Value (Amount per Serving):

Calories 196

Fat 17.8 g

Carbohydrates 7.3 g

Sugar 2.7 g

Protein 3.2 g

Cholesterol 51 mg

63-Mushroom Garlic Bok Choy

Total Time: 15 minutes

Serving Size: 2

Ingredients:

- 10 oz bok Choy, rinsed, drained, and chopped
- 4 oz mushrooms, sliced
- 3 garlic cloves, minced
- 1 1/2 tbsp olive oil
- 1/4 tsp salt

Directions:

Heat oil in the pan over high heat.

Add garlic, mushroom, salt, and Bok Choy and sauté until Bok Choy wilted.

Remove from heat and serve immediately and enjoy.

Nutritional Value (Amount per Serving):

Calories 146

Fat 10.6 g

Carbohydrates 12.4 g

Sugar 3.8 g

Protein 3.3 g

Cholesterol 0 mg

DAY 22

64-Easy Cream Cheese Pancakes

Total Time: 15 minutes

Serving Size: 4

Ingredients:

- 2 eggs
- 1/2 tsp cinnamon
- 1 tsp granulated sweetener
- 2 oz cream cheese

Directions:

Add all ingredients into the blender and blend until smooth.

Heat pan over medium heat.

Spray pan with cooking spray.

Pour batter into the hot pan and make small pancake and cook pancake until lightly golden brown from both the sides.

Serve and enjoy.

Nutritional Value (Amount per Serving):

Calories 82

Fat 7.1 g

Carbohydrates 0.8 g

Sugar 0.2 g

Protein 3.9 g

Cholesterol 97 mg

65-Broccoli Spinach Coconut Curry

Total Time: 40 minutes

Serving Size: 4

Ingredients:

- 1/2 cup coconut cream
- 1/4 onion, sliced
- 4 tbsp coconut oil
- 1/2 cup spinach
- 1 cup broccoli florets
- 1 tbsp red curry paste
- 2 tsp soy sauce
- 1 tsp ginger, minced
- 1 tsp garlic, minced

Directions:

Heat 2 tbsp coconut oil to a pan over medium-high heat.
Add onion and cook until softened.

Add garlic and sauté for minutes.

Reduce heat to medium-low and add broccoli and stir
everything well.

Once broccoli is cooked then move vegetables to the
other side of the pan.

Add curry paste and cook for a minute.

Add spinach and cook until wilted.

Add coconut cream, remaining oil, ginger, and soy
sauce. Stir well and simmer for 5 minutes.

Serve and enjoy.

Nutritional Value (Amount per Serving):

Calories 228

Fat 23.1 g

Carbohydrates 5.9 g

Sugar 1.9 g

Protein 2.1 g

Cholesterol 0 mg

66-Creamy Cheese Asparagus

Total Time: 25 minutes

Serving Size: 4

Ingredients:

- 1 lb asparagus, wash and trim off the ends
- 1 cup mozzarella cheese, shredded
- 1/2 cup asiago cheese, grated
- 1 tbsp Italian seasoning
- 1 cup heavy whipping cream
- Pepper
- Salt

Directions:

Preheat the oven to 400 F.

Spray baking dish with cooking spray and set aside.

Place asparagus into the prepared baking dish.

In a small bowl, whisk together heavy cream, asiago cheese, Italian seasoning, pepper, and salt.

Pour heavy cream mixture over the asparagus.

Sprinkle with shredded mozzarella cheese.

Bake in preheated oven for 18 minutes.

Serve and enjoy.

Nutritional Value (Amount per Serving):

Calories 214

Fat 18.2 g

Carbohydrates 6.1 g

Sugar 2.5 g

Protein 8.6 g

Cholesterol 62 mg

DAY 23

67-Quick Mug Scramble

Total Time: 5 minutes

Serving Size: 1

Ingredients:

- 2 eggs
- 2 tbsp Colby jack cheese, shredded
- 1 tbsp almond milk
- Pepper
- Salt

Directions:

Spray microwave safe mug with cooking spray.

Add eggs, milk, pepper, and salt into the mug and whisk well.

Microwave egg mixture on high for 45 seconds. Stir well.

Add cheese and microwave for 5 seconds.

Serve and enjoy.

Nutritional Value (Amount per Serving):

Calories 215

Fat 16.8 g

Carbohydrates 2 g

Sugar 1.2 g

Protein 14.4 g

Cholesterol 340 mg

68-Creamy Spinach

Total Time: 25 minutes

Serving Size: 3

Ingredients:

- 10 oz frozen spinach
- 1/4 tsp onion powder
- 1/4 tsp garlic powder
- 2 tbsp sour cream
- 3 oz cream cheese
- 3 tbsp parmesan cheese
- Pepper
- Salt

Directions:

Heat pan over medium-high heat.

Add spinach and some water boil off.

Season spinach with onion powder, garlic powder, pepper, and salt.

Add cream cheese and stir until cheese is melted.

Add sour cream and stir well.

Reduce heat to low and add parmesan cheese. Stir until spinach is thickened.

Serve and enjoy.

Nutritional Value (Amount per Serving):

Calories 160

Fat 13.3 g

Carbohydrates 5 g

Sugar 0.6 g

Protein 7 g

Cholesterol 38 mg

69-Creamy Parmesan Asparagus Soup

Total Time: 15 minutes

Serving Size: 4

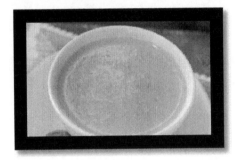

Ingredients:

- 1/2 cup heavy whipping cream
- 2 oz parmesan cheese, shredded
- 4 garlic cloves, minced
- 2 lbs asparagus, trimmed and cut into pieces
- 1 small onion, chopped
- 2 tbsp butter
- 4 cups vegetable broth
- 1/2 tsp salt

Directions:

Add broth into the large microwave safe bowl and microwave on high for 5 minutes.

Melt butter in a large pot over low heat.

Add chopped onion, garlic, salt, and asparagus to the pot and saute for 5 minutes.

Add broth and bring to boil. Reduce heat and simmer for 2-3 minutes or until tender.

Using blender puree the soup until smooth.

Add cream. Stir well and heat over medium heat.

Remove pot from eating and stir in parmesan cheese.

Serve and enjoy.

Nutritional Value (Amount per Serving):

Calories 205

Fat 14.7 g

Carbohydrates 12.4 g

Sugar 5.1 g

Protein 10.3 g

Cholesterol 46 mg

DAY 24

70-Delicious Pumpkin Spice Porridge

Total Time: 15 minutes

Serving Size: 1

Ingredients:

- 1 large egg, beaten
- 1/2 tsp pumpkin pie spice
- 3/4 cup water
- 1 tbsp flax meal
- 2 tbsp almond flour
- Pinch of salt
- Top with:
- 1 tbsp butter
- 1 tbsp heavy cream

- 1 tbsp granulated sweetener
- 2 tbsp can pumpkin
- 1 tsp vanilla extract

Directions:

Add almond flour, flax meal, water, pumpkin pie spice, and salt into the pot and heat over medium-high heat. Once mixture begins to simmer then reduce the heat to medium. Whisk until thickens.

Remove pot from heat and slowly add egg and whisk well.

Again place the pot on medium heat and whisk until porridge thickens.

Remove pot from heat and whisk in remaining ingredients.

Serve and enjoy.

Nutritional Value (Amount per Serving):

Calories 365

Fat 31.6 g

Carbohydrates 10.2 g

Sugar 2.9 g

Protein 11.6 g

Cholesterol 237 mg

71-Yummy Cauliflower Mac and Cheese

Total Time: 30 minutes

Serving Size: 4

Ingredients:

- 1 cup heavy cream
- 1/8 tsp garlic powder
- 1/4 tsp black pepper
- 2 cups cheddar cheese, shredded
- 1 tsp Dijon mustard
- 2 oz cream cheese
- 1 large cauliflower head, cut into florets
- 1/2 tsp kosher salt

Directions:

Preheat the oven to 375 F.

Add water and salt to the pot and bring to boil.

Spray baking dish with cooking spray and set aside.

Add cauliflower florets into the boiling water and cook about 5 minutes. Drain well and transfer to baking dish.

Add cream into the saucepan and bring to simmer, whisk in mustard and cream cheese until smooth.

Stir in 1 1/2 cup cheese, pepper, garlic, and salt. Whisk until cheese melts for 2 minutes.

Season with pepper and salt.

Remove pan from heat and pour over cauliflower florets and stir well.

Top with remaining cheese and bake in preheated oven for 15 minutes.

Serve and enjoy.

Nutritional Value (Amount per Serving):

Calories 435

Fat 35 g

Carbohydrates 13 g

Sugar 5.4 g

Protein 20 g

Cholesterol 116 mg

72-Cucumber Cheese Salad

Total Time: 15 minutes

Serving Size: 4

Ingredients:

- 2 cups cucumbers, chopped
- 1/2 cup feta cheese, crumbled
- 1/2 cup fresh mint, chopped
- 1 tbsp lime juice
- 2 ripe avocados, peeled and chopped
- 1/4 tsp salt
- For dressing:
- 2 tbsp olive oil

Directions:

In a bowl, add chopped cucumbers and salt and set aside for 20 minutes.

Drain cucumber liquid then adds all remaining ingredients and stir well.

Serve and enjoy.

Nutritional Value (Amount per Serving):

Calories 328

Fat 30.7 g

Carbohydrates 12.3 g

Sugar 2.1 g

Protein 5.3 g

Cholesterol 17 mg

DAY 25

73-Healthy Spinach Cheese Eggs

Total Time: 35 minutes

Serving Size: 2

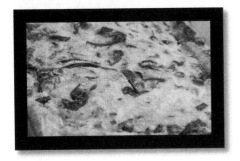

Ingredients:

- 3 eggs
- 1/4 cup almond milk
- 1/4 cup parmesan cheese
- 3 oz spinach, chopped
- 3 oz cottage cheese

Directions:

Preheat the oven to 375 F.

Spray baking dish with cooking spray.

In a bowl, whisk together egg, milk, parmesan cheese, and cottage cheese.

Add spinach and stir well.

Pour egg mixture into the baking dish and bake in preheated oven for 25 minutes.

Serve and enjoy.

Nutritional Value (Amount per Serving):

Calories 377

Fat 25.6 g

Carbohydrates 6.6 g

Sugar 1.8 g

Protein 31.2 g

Cholesterol 278 mg

74-Delicious Marinated Eggplant

Total Time: 60 minutes

Serving Size: 6

Ingredients:

- 2 large eggplant, cut into 1/4 inch slices
- 2 garlic cloves, chopped
- 1/4 cup fresh mint, chopped
- 1 tbsp vinegar
- 4.5 tbsp olive oil
- 1 tbsp oregano
- 1/2 red chili
- Salt

Directions:

Add sliced eggplant into the mixing bowl.

Sprinkle a little salt over the slices eggplant and set aside for 30 minutes to release some water.

Rinse eggplant well and pat dry with paper towel.

Brush eggplant with oil.

Place eggplant slices on the hot griddle pan and cook until softened.

In a small bowl, mix together all remaining ingredients and set aside.

Arrange cooked eggplant slices on serving dish and drizzle marinade over the eggplant slices.

Serve and enjoy.

Nutritional Value (Amount per Serving):

Calories 134

Fat 10 g

Carbohydrates 10 g

Sugar 4 g

Protein 1 g

Cholesterol 0 mg

75-Creamy Cucumber Avocado Egg Salad

Total Time: 15 minutes

Serving Size: 4

Ingredients:

- 6 hard-boiled eggs, peel and diced
- 1/2 tsp paprika
- 1/4 cup mayo
- 1 large avocado, peel and chopped
- 1 cucumber, peel and chopped
- Salt

Directions:

Add all ingredients into the large mixing bowl and mix well until combined.

Serve and enjoy.

Nutritional Value (Amount per Serving):

Calories 266

Fat 21.4 g

Carbohydrates 11.2 g

Sugar 3 g

Protein 9.9 g

Cholesterol 249 mg

<u>DAY 26</u>

76-Egg Cream Cheese Casserole

Total Time: 35 minutes

Serving Size: 2

Ingredients:

- 5 eggs
- 2 tbsp parmesan cheese, grated
- 2 tbsp heavy cream
- 3 tbsp tomato sauce

Directions:

Preheat the oven to 350 F.

Spray baking dish with cooking spray.

In a mixing bowl, mix together eggs and cream.

Add cheese and tomato sauce. Mix well.

Pour egg mixture into the baking dish and bake in preheated oven for 25-30 minutes.

Serve and enjoy.

Nutritional Value (Amount per Serving):

Calories 235

Fat 17.9 g

Carbohydrates 2.7 g

Sugar 1.9 g

Protein 16.3 g

Cholesterol 433 mg

77-Stir Fried Garlic Eggplant

Total Time: 35 minutes

Serving Size: 4

Ingredients:

- 4 cups eggplant, sliced
- 1 green pepper, sliced
- 2 garlic cloves, minced
- 1 medium onion, chopped
- 1/2 tsp ground ginger
- 1 tsp red pepper flakes
- 6 tbsp tamari sauce
- 1 tbsp olive oil

Directions:

Add olive into the pan and heat over medium-high heat.

Add onion and garlic into the pan and cook for 6 to 8 minutes.

Reduce heat to medium and add eggplant and green pepper. Stir well and cook for few minutes.

Add red pepper flakes, ginger, and tamari and stir well.

Cook eggplant mixture for 12 minutes. Stir occasionally.

Serve and enjoy.

Nutritional Value (Amount per Serving):

Calories 88

Fat 3 g

Carbohydrates 11 g

Sugar 4 g

Protein 4 g

Cholesterol 0 mg

78-Baked Zucchini with herbs

Total Time: 45 minutes

Serving Size: 6

Ingredients:

- 2 1/2 lbs zucchini, cut into quarters
- 1/3 cup parsley, chopped
- 1 tsp dried basil
- 1/2 cup parmesan cheese, shredded
- 6 garlic cloves, crushed
- 10 oz cherry tomatoes cut in half
- 1/2 tsp black pepper
- 3/4 tsp salt

Directions:

Preheat the oven to 350 F.

Spray baking dish with cooking spray and set aside.

Add all ingredients except parsley into the large mixing bowl and stir well to combine.

Pour egg mixture into the prepared baking dish.

Bake in preheated oven for 35 minutes.

Garnish with parsley and serve.

Nutritional Value (Amount per Serving):

Calories 106

Fat 4.3 g

Carbohydrates 10.6 g

Sugar 4.5 g

Protein 8.2 g

Cholesterol 10 mg

DAY 27

79-Quick Spanish omelet

Total Time: 15 minutes

Serving Size: 2

Ingredients:

- 3 eggs
- 1/2 bell pepper, chopped
- 1/2 onion chopped
- 1 tbsp parsley, chopped
- 1/4 cup spinach, chopped
- 1/4 tsp cayenne pepper
- 1 tsp extra virgin olive oil
- 1/4 tsp black pepper
- 1/4 tsp salt

Directions:

Heat olive oil in a pan over medium heat.

Add vegetables to the pan and sauté until softened.

In another bowl, whisk together eggs, cayenne, pepper, and salt.

Pour egg mixture into the hot pan and cook until set.

Once almost cooked then top with sautéed vegetables and flip heat through.

Serve and enjoy.

Nutritional Value (Amount per Serving):

Calories 138

Fat 9.1 g

Carbohydrates 5.9 g

Sugar 3.2 g

Protein 9.1 g

Cholesterol 246 mg

80-Eggplant Spinach Salad

Total Time: 30 minutes

Serving Size: 4

Ingredients:

- 1 tbsp oregano, chopped
- 1 tbsp parsley, chopped
- 1 tbsp fresh mint, chopped
- 1 large eggplant, cut into 3/4 inch slices
- 5 oz spinach
- 1 tbsp sun-dried tomatoes, chopped
- 1 tbsp shallot, chopped
- For dressing:
- 1/4 cup olive oil
- 1/2 lemon juice
- 1/2 tsp smoked paprika

- 1 tsp Dijon mustard
- 1 tsp tahini
- 2 garlic cloves, minced
- Pepper
- Salt

Directions:

Place sliced eggplants into the large bowl and sprinkle with salt and set aside for minutes.

For salad dressing: in a small bowl mix together all dressing ingredients. Set aside.

Heat grill to medium-high heat.

In a large salad bowl, add shallot, sun-dried tomatoes, herbs, and spinach.

Rinse eggplant slices and pat dry with paper towel.

Brush eggplant slices with olive oil and grill on medium high heat for 3-4 minutes on each side.

Let cool the grilled eggplant slices then cut into quarters.

Add eggplant to the salad bowl and pour dressing over salad. Toss well.

Serve and enjoy.

Nutritional Value (Amount per Serving):

Calories 163

Fat 13 g

Carbohydrates 10 g

Sugar 3 g

Protein 2 g

Cholesterol 0 mg

81-Cheesy Zucchini Casserole

Total Time: 35 minutes

Serving Size: 6

Ingredients:

- 4 cup zucchini, grated
- 1/2 cup cheddar cheese, shredded
- 1 cup mozzarella cheese, shredded
- 1/2 cup parmesan cheese, grated
- 2 eggs
- 1 tbsp garlic, minced
- 1/2 cup onion, diced
- 1/2 tsp salt

Directions:

Preheat the oven to 375 F.

Spray baking dish with cooking spray and set aside.

Add zucchini and salt into the colander and set aside for 10 minutes.

After 10 minutes squeeze out all liquid from zucchini.

Combine together zucchini, cheddar cheese, mozzarella cheese, 1/2 parmesan cheese, eggs, garlic, and onion and pour into the prepared baking dish.

Bake in preheated oven for 25 minutes.

Serve and enjoy.

Nutritional Value (Amount per Serving):

Calories 146

Fat 9.2 g

Carbohydrates 4.7 g

Sugar 1.9 g

Protein 11.7 g

Cholesterol 77 mg

DAY 28

82-Perfect Egg Scrambled

Total Time: 15 minutes

Serving Size: 1

Ingredients:

- 3 eggs
- 1 tbsp butter
- 2 tbsp sour cream
- 1/4 tsp black pepper
- 1/4 tsp sea salt

Directions:

In a bowl, whisk eggs with pepper and salt.
Melt butter in a pan over medium heat.

Once butter is melted then pour egg mixture into the pan and stir constantly.

When eggs are cooked then remove from heat and stir in sour cream.

Serve and enjoy.

Nutritional Value (Amount per Serving):

Calories 343

Fat 29.7 g

Carbohydrates 2.4 g

Sugar 1.1 g

Protein 17.6 g

Cholesterol 532 mg

83-Spicy Eggplant with Jalapeno pepper

Total Time: 6 hours 40 minutes

Serving Size: 4

Ingredients:

- 1.5 lbs eggplant, cut into 1/ 4 inch sliced
- 1 large bell pepper, roasted and diced
- 1/2 jalapeno pepper, seeded and chopped
- 3/4 cup olive oil
- 1 tbsp parsley, chopped
- 1.5 tsp capers, drained, rinsed and chopped
- 1 garlic clove, minced
- 1/4 tsp black peppers
- 1 tsp kosher salt

Directions:

Place eggplant slices into the bowl and sprinkle with salt. Set aside for 30 minutes.

After 30 minutes rinse eggplant and pat dry with paper towel.

Brush eggplant with 1/4 cup olive oil.

Heat pan over medium heat.

Add eggplant to the pan and cook until golden brown on both the sides.

Arrange cooked eggplant slices into the casserole dish and season with pepper and salt.

Mix together parsley, capers, garlic, pepper, jalapeno and remaining olive oil in a bowl.

Pour parsley mixture over the eggplant slices.

Cover dish and set aside for 6 hours.

Serve and enjoy.

Nutritional Value (Amount per Serving):

Calories 379

Fat 38 g

Carbohydrates 12 g

Sugar 6 g

Protein 2 g

Cholesterol 0 mg

84-Easy Pan Zucchini and Squash

Total Time: 15 minutes

Serving Size: 2

Ingredients:

- 2 tbsp parmesan cheese, shredded
- 2 medium yellow squash, diced
- 2 small zucchini, trimmed and diced
- 1/2 tbsp olive oil
- 1/2 tbsp butter
- Pepper
- Salt

Directions:

Heat olive oil in a pan over medium heat.

Add squash and zucchini into the pan and season with pepper and salt. Let sit for 2 minutes.

Stir well and cook until lightly golden brown, about 6-7 minutes.

Top with shredded parmesan cheese and serve.

Nutritional Value (Amount per Serving):

Calories 126

Fat 8.3 g

Carbohydrates 10.7 g

Sugar 6.4 g

Protein 5.7 g

Cholesterol 11 mg

DAY 29

85-Delicious Coconut Porridge

Total Time: 15 minutes

Serving Size: 1

Ingredients:

- 4 tbsp coconut cream
- 1 tbsp coconut flour
- 1 egg
- 1 oz butter
- Pinch of salt

Directions:

Add all ingredients into the saucepan and mix well.

Heat porridge mixture over low heat. Stir constantly until you get desired texture.

Serve with coconut milk and top with fresh berries.

Nutritional Value (Amount per Serving):

Calories 464

Fat 43.7 g

Carbohydrates 11.7 g

Sugar 3.4 g

Protein 9.2 g

Cholesterol 225 mg

86-Grilled Eggplant Zucchini

Total Time: 1 hour 10 minutes

Serving Size: 8

Ingredients:

- 3 zucchinis, cut into 1/2 inch slices
- 2 green bell peppers, cut into 1/2 inch slices
- 2 eggplants, cut into 1/2 inch slices
- 1/2 cup olive oil
- 2 tbsp soy sauce
- 2 tbsp balsamic vinegar
- 1/2 tsp ground black pepper
- 1/2 tsp salt

Directions:

In a large bowl, whisk together vinegar, soy sauce, olive oil, pepper, and salt.

Toss bell peppers, zucchinis, and eggplants in soy sauce mixture and marinate for 45 minutes.

Preheat the grill over medium heat.

Lightly grease the grill with oil.

Remove vegetables from marinade and place on a preheated grill and grill for 15 minutes.

Serve and enjoy.

Nutritional Value (Amount per Serving):

Calories 167

Fat 13 g

Carbohydrates 13 g

Sugar 7 g

Protein 2 g

Cholesterol 0 mg

87-Healthy Zucchini Noodles

Total Time: 15 minutes

Serving Size: 4

Ingredients:

- 4 small zucchini, end trimmed
- 1/4 cup parmesan cheese, grated
- 2 tsp lemon juice
- 1/3 cup extra-virgin olive oil
- 2 garlic cloves
- 2 cups fresh basil leaves
- Pepper
- Salt

Directions:

Using vegetable peeler slice zucchini into the noodles and set aside.

Add garlic, basil, olive oil, parmesan cheese, and lemon juice into the food processor and pulse until well blended. Season with pepper and salt.

In a large bowl, combine together pesto and zucchini noodles.

Serve and enjoy.

Nutritional Value (Amount per Serving):

Calories 188

Fat 18.1 g

Carbohydrates 4.8 g

Sugar 2.2 g

Protein 3.9 g

Cholesterol 6 mg

DAY 30

88-Perfect Keto Latte

Total Time: 5 minutes

Serving Size: 2

Ingredients:

- 2 eggs
- 1 tsp pumpkin pie spice
- 1/2 tsp vanilla extract
- 1 1/2 cup boiling water
- 2 tbsp coconut oil

Directions:

Add all ingredients into the blender and blend until smooth.

Serve immediately and enjoy.

Nutritional Value (Amount per Serving):

Calories 185
Fat 18.1 g
Carbohydrates 1 g
Sugar 0.5 g
Protein 5.6 g
Cholesterol 164 mg

89-Roasted Squash with Lemon

Total Time: 1 hour 10 minutes

Serving Size: 3

Ingredients:

- 2 lbs summer squash, cut into 1-inch pieces
- 1 large lemon
- 1/8 tsp paprika
- 1/8 tsp pepper
- 1/8 tsp garlic powder
- 3 tbsp olive oil
- Pepper
- Salt

Directions:

Preheat the oven to 400 F.

Spray a baking tray with cooking spray.

Place squash pieces onto the prepared baking tray and drizzle with olive oil.

Season with paprika, pepper, and garlic powder.

Squeeze lemon juice over the squash and bake in preheated oven for 50-60 minutes.

Serve immediately and enjoy.

Nutritional Value (Amount per Serving):

Calories 184

Fat 14.9 g

Carbohydrates 13 g

Sugar 11 g

Protein 3.3 g

Cholesterol 0 mg

90-Creamy Squash Coconut Curry Soup

Total Time: 35 minutes

Serving Size: 4

Ingredients:

- 1 1/2 lbs summer squash, ends trimmed and cut into 1-inch pieces
- 1/2 lime juice
- 1/4 cup coconut milk
- 4 cups vegetable stock
- 3/4 tsp curry powder
- 1 garlic clove, minced
- 1 onion, chopped
- 1 tbsp olive oil
- Pepper

- Salt

Directions:

Heat olive oil in the large pot over medium heat.

Add onion to the pot and sauté for 8 minutes.

Add curry powder and garlic and sauté for 30 seconds.

Add squash and sauté for 2 minutes.

Add stock and bring to boil.

Reduce heat to medium-low and simmer for 15 minutes.

Using blender puree the soup until smooth.

Stir in lime juice and coconut milk.

Season with pepper and salt.

Serve and enjoy.

Nutritional Value (Amount per Serving):

Calories 114

Fat 8.1 g

Carbohydrates 11.5 g

Sugar 8.3 g

Protein 2.5 g

Cholesterol 0 mg

63516540R00106

Made in the USA
Middletown, DE
01 February 2018